FOREX MONEY MANAGEMENT

AND

RISK MANAGEMENT

I0446446

A practical guide on how to minimize your risk and

maximize your profit in forex trading, understanding

how to use proper lot size and setting logical exit point

Abraham Robert. C

In order to say thank you for purchasing this book, I offer the below video course and more to you as a token of appreciation

Find the Link to the bonus video courses at the end of the book

TABLE OF CONTENT

CHAPTER 1

Forex money management

A common mistake made by traders is to ignore the importance of forex money management. To their detriment, traders who disregard money management in Forex do so out of ignorance or laziness. Effective money management is, in fact, one of the things that separates successful traders from losers most of the time.

To put it simply, Forex money management refers to a set of self-imposed guidelines that profitable traders adhere to in order to efficiently manage their finances, limiting losses, maximizing

gains, and expanding the size of their trading account.

Given how similar the two ideas are, it seems sense that risk management and forex money management are frequently conflated.

The main goal of risk management is to efficiently identify, assess, and quantify all of the dangers involved in trading so that you can shield yourself from its drawbacks. The only goal of money management is to keep your money safe.

The classic trading maxim "cut your losses short and let your winners run" serves as a good way to summarize the goal of money management. Put another way, reduce losses, maximum earnings, and ideally you'll achieve this to become a lucrative, successful Forex trader.

Effective money management is crucial while trading forex. If one did not practice appropriate risk and money management, trading would resemble casino gambling rather than stand out all that much. If a trader disregards even the most basic money management principles, then even the most successful trading method will not provide lucrative trading outcomes.

Effective money management is crucial while trading forex. If one did not practice appropriate risk and money management, trading would resemble casino gambling rather than stand out all that much. If a trader disregards even the most basic money management principles, then even the most successful trading method will not provide lucrative trading outcomes.

A collection of strategies used to increase your trading account's growth, minimize losses, and maximize profits is referred to as money management.

Forex Money Management Strategies

Risk only the amount you are willing to lose on a trade

Traders should only trade with money they can afford to lose, which brings us to our first and perhaps most crucial money management advice for Forex.

You should never put more money into your trading account than you can afford to lose as a trader.

Consider establishing a monthly maximum allowable loss for yourself, and if you reach it, quit trading right away. The concept is that you are only taking a chance with money that, should you lose it, won't significantly alter your life. Never exchange money that you require for necessities such as rent, a mortgage, groceries, transportation to work, etc.

Trading forex is not a certain way to gain money. Some traders will only have losses at the conclusion of their Forex careers. Never put at danger more than you can afford.

Calculate the Risk for Each Trade

Establishing how much you are going to risk every transaction and how you are going to measure it is the next stage in developing your Forex money management plan, once you have determined how much money you are comfortable trading with.

This will assist you in deciding where to put your stop loss each time you get into the market.

There are two popular approaches to risk quantification, both having pros and cons.

Fixed Amount

Some traders establish a fixed monetary maximum risk each deal. A trader may, for instance, deposit £10,000 into their trading account and decide to risk £500 on each transaction.

It is fairly simple to abide by this guideline. You are fully aware of the risk involved in every deal, regardless of its nature. You can figure out without much computation that if you make ten transactions a day, your total risk will be £5,000.

This strategy's drawback is that it doesn't account for variations in your trading balance.

You might not be getting as much return if you have a run of winning trades and significantly increase your account balance while maintaining the same level of risk on each deal.

Conversely, you are risking a larger percentage of your account, which might cause your balance to decrease much faster, if you lose a lot of trades while your risk per deal stays at £500.

A Fixed Percentage

The most popular strategy is to risk a certain proportion of your account balance with every deal. Consequently, the first transaction would risk £200 if a trader with a £10,000 account balance decided they wanted to risk 2% of their capital per trade.

The advantage of incorporating this technique into your Forex money management plan is that, in contrast to employing a fixed amount, your risk per transaction will change in tandem with the balance of your account.

Theoretically, if it is adhered to, you could never lose your whole account balance, and while you are winning a lot of money, you raise your risk to benefit from the greater quantity of available cash.

The drawback is that your risk per transaction will decrease over time along with your balance if you do experience a string of losses.

This implies that it will take you longer to recover your investment if and when you begin to make winning transactions.

Determine the Ratio of Risk to Reward.

Now that you are aware of the amount you want to risk on each transaction, determine the amount you hope to make from that risk and use that information to assist you set a take-profit price for your deals.

Your trading style and, in particular, your risk tolerance will determine this decision. If your maximum allowable loss is $100, your profit objective would likewise be $100 if your risk to reward ratio is 1:1. Nonetheless, a ratio of 1:3 would result in a goal profit of $300 for the same level of risk.

It is widely acknowledged that a risk to reward ratio ought to exceed a ratio of 1:1. This is due to the fact that if your risk to reward ratio was 1:1 and you made three consecutive wins and three consecutive losses, you would have lost £0 overall.

On the other hand, if you were trading with a 1:2 risk to reward ratio and you had three wins and three losses, you would still be in the black as your profit was more than the losses on each deal.

Understand currency relationships

Forex money management methods and investment plans should both recognize and capitalize on currency connections. The degree to which one pair of currencies will move in tandem with another is indicated by currency correlations. A Forex trading portfolio that diversifies the overall trading risk should be created using the correlation coefficient, which has a range of -1 to 1.

Utilize trailing stops to secure your earnings

Different kinds of stop loss orders for different kinds of market scenarios should be part of a well-designed money management strategy for Forex trading. It might make sense to employ a trailing stop placed at the average height of the corrective wave if the market is in a strong trend. By doing this, you'll be able to lock in winnings during the trend as the trailing stop will automatically adjust your stop loss.

Don't have greed

Among the most destructive emotions in trading are greed and fear. As you gain expertise, you'll be able to control your emotions and prevent them from influencing your trade choices. It is important to be realistic about what you can extract from the market since greed may be particularly destructive. Avoid making excessive trades in the market and establishing unattainable profit goals. A trade with a 1,000-pip profit objective and a 10-pip stop loss will probably end in loss.

Don't trade the market too much

It's not necessary for you to trade every hour or even every day. Don't pursue the market for trading chances; instead, wait for the trade setup to materialize. You owe the market nothing, and the secret to successful trading is patience and discipline.

If you make several transactions without conducting any market research, not even the greatest Forex money management system will be of much use to you.

Make the correct position size calculation

Many traders lack the knowledge necessary to determine their position size accurately in order to maintain their specified risk-per-trade. Since position sizes determine the possible profit on a trade, they are important in Forex money management.

Reduce your losses and allow your profits to run

"Cut your losses short and let your profits run" is a statement you may be familiar with if you've followed foreign Forex trading advice. That is exactly what professional Forex traders do; they let their winning positions run while being extremely impatient with their losses and closing a losing position early. The converse is true for novices to the market; they cut short their earnings out of concern that they will be lost and let their losses continue in the hopes that they will turn around.

Always use Stop Loss orders

Any Forex money management strategy should include stop loss orders as they are a crucial component of risk and money management. In order to limit bigger losses, a stop loss order automatically cancels your trade when the price hits a certain threshold. Stop Loss orders are an essential component of any money management strategy used in Forex trading. Honor Leverage

Forex traders can open greater bets using leverage than they normally could with their funds. In essence, the trader is opening a leveraged position by borrowing money from their broker.

With a leverage of 1:20, for instance, a trader may initiate a position for £10,000 with just £500 in their account.

It seems like a terrific offer, and if you utilize it well, it may help you become a profitable trader. Leverage may increase returns on your profitable trades by enabling you to acquire a larger position with less money.

Leverage, however—and this is crucial—has two drawbacks. When a deal goes bad, the amplified gains from successful trades turn into amplified losses. As a result, it's critical to employ leverage carefully and respectfully.

Take Profit Out

A common mistake made by traders is to either not take their profits out of the market at all or not often enough.

If you begin to see a sizable return on your trading account, take some money out, enjoy it, and use it for a worthy endeavor.

As we mentioned at the outset, optimizing your profit is a component of Forex money management. Taking care of your profit when you have one is necessary for you to do this. You are more likely to trade with the money and maybe lose it if it is left in your trading account for an extended period of time.

You need a well-defined trading strategy

Before executing any trades, it is vital to have a clear trading plan. In order to avoid aggressive and unpredictable trading, which frequently ends in losses, establish the entry and exit spots, targeted yield, and acceptable loss percentages.

Trade only instruments with high liquidity

To avoid losses, focus on trading instruments that are leading the marketplace.

Trading ought to take place around strong pivot point.

Don't trade because you're bored or impatient. Though it's not an exact science, a few traders use oscillators and indicators to identify strong turning points on the chart. Not everyone can gain experience and intuition, which are necessary for mastering this ability.

You must avoid trades in smaller timeframes

Although there are short-term trading tactics, such as scalping, they are difficult to implement and effectively manage. Strive for profits while trading which are at least ten times greater than the commission expenses. Never try to earn money on every movement in the market.

Buy low, sell high

The price might change in either way, so keep that in mind. Understanding of the foreign exchange market can increase your likelihood of succeeding, but it cannot ensure success.

Avoid making trading decision at the end of the trading day

It is not a lucrative strategy to trade just before the market shuts, such as on a Friday or at the conclusion of the trading day.

Master both technical and fundamental analysis

Strong analytical skills are essential to your trading success. Consider it like to a detective looking into a case.

Technical analysis, which involves deciphering charts and indicators, and fundamental analysis, which involves examining market news and economic issues, both require improvement.

Maintain a trade log

Consider it your own trading logbook. It's a useful tool for trading reflection and performance improvement going forward.

Don't enter or exit trades too often

If you regularly open and close trades on a regular basis, it might work against you. It is like trying to catch an insect with a net that has numerous holes; you will not succeed in capturing anything. Wait for high-probability chances with patience.

Don't trade against the trend

According to experts, trends can help you trade successfully. Although defying the trend can sometimes be rewarding, it's a hazardous strategy.

Don't try to predict trend reversal

Despite using a variety of instruments and indicators, analysts find it difficult to reliably pinpoint pivot points. Spend no time on this. Aim for a high success rate rather than being correct all the time.

Never use averaging

That's going to hurt your trading account. Even if it might be alluring to average up or down for a little while, doing so frequently results in large losses. In an uptrend or in the foreign exchange market, averaging downward might be particularly risky.

Keep what you gain

Treat the money you make with dignity. Recall that this is your hard-earned cash. Avoid taking unnecessary risks in the market even with the profit you make.

Live an active life

Avoid staying in front of your laptop all the time. Take part in physical activities, such as attending a gym or playing sports. It's critical to lead a balanced life.

Easily accept losses

Reduce your losses to a manageable level and accept them. Instead, concentrate on generating significant earnings. For the purpose of to minimize potential losses, some traders use pyramiding, in which they increase positions one after another while additionally placing stop orders in place. Because losing or zero deals are a part of the market's inevitable ups and downs, be ready for them.

CHAPTER 2

RISK MANAGEMENT

A trading plans, ability to incorporate risk management techniques can distinguish between legitimate trading and gambling. A trader may begin to lose money when deals are made without taking risk into account.

Taking measured risks is the foundation of trading; the goal is to reduce losses while increasing gains.

Risk Management Advice

- Set take targets level using a proper risk reward ratio
- Don't let your feelings influence your trading selections.
- Determine the anticipated return.

Setting stop losses, determining the ideal position size, and exercising emotional restraint while entering and leaving trades are a few examples of risk management techniques.

Essentials of Managing Foreign Exchange Risk

Appetite for Risk

A key component of effective foreign exchange risk management is figuring out your level of risk tolerance. For extremely volatile currencies, like some developing market currencies, this is very important. In addition, in forex trading, liquidity plays an essential part in managing risks since less liquid currency pairs can make it harder to open and exit positions at the price you want.

Your position size may end up being excessive if you don't know how much you can lose. This might lead to losses that make it harder for you to take on the next trade, or worse.

Assume that half of your transactions are profitable. In the long run, it is theoretically expected that there will be streaks of consecutive losses in trading. The probabilities indicate that at some time over a trading career of 10,000 deals, you will experience 13 consecutive losses. This highlights how important it is to understand your capacity for risk because you need to have enough money in your account to get through tough times.

So, what level of risk is appropriate? It's generally advisable to risk no more than 1% to 2% of your account balance pair trade.

Cut off losses

Understanding stop loss orders is crucial for good risk management in forex trading, since they are used to terminate a transaction at a designated price.

Leverage

With leverage in forex, traders can expose themselves more than their trading account could normally permit, increasing both the potential for profit and the danger. As such, leverage needs to be handled properly.

Managing Your Feelings while trading

You should be able to control your emotions while trading in any financial market where you are risking your money.

Keeping a forex trading notebook or record can help you develop your methods based on past facts, not on your sentiments, and help you trade objectively by removing your emotions from the equation.

Size of Position

It is crucial to choose the proper position size, or the amount of lots you take on a trade, as it will safeguard your account and optimize prospects. You have to determine your stop location, determine your risk percent, and estimate your lot size and pips cost in order to determine the appropriate position size.

You must acknowledge that you will be dealing with risk when you trade forex or CFDs and accept this as a requirement before you can trade. While trading entails many dangers, there are a number of strategies to lower these risks.

How to effectively manage risk

- Practice positions sizing
- Understand your trading risks.
- Examine and assess these risks.
- Determine ways to lower these risks.
- Apply and oversee such fixes consistently.

Position scaling may be tackled in a variety of ways, from the most basic to the most intricate, depending on what works best for your platform. In this manner, managing winning and losing transactions is made simple for you.

Models To Manage You Winning and Losing Transaction

Fixed-size lot

Excellent method for new traders to begin their careers. This implies that traders will likely trade with modest positions at all. During a trade, lots might be adjusted based on how the account balance changes during the trading session.

When first starting off, it's crucial to have a modest account with a 2:1 leverage ratio so that you may gradually increase your potential income over time.

Equity Share

The concept behind Equity Percent depends on how much of a change in equity % determines the size of your stake. As this will decide and allow for growth of equity in proportion to position size, it is important to ascertain the percentage of equity for each position.

It is always possible to raise the proportion of equity employed in each trade, but it should be noted that bigger potential profits come with more risk.

What percentage of equity is safe to trade

It is often recommended to trade with a lower equity proportion, like 1% or 2%, which translates to 50:1 leverage every transaction and also enables you to hold onto your position for an extended amount of time. To put it simply, make transactions that are proportionate to your equity.

If you lose, you lower the size of your position to prevent the account from rapidly emptying to zero. To lessen the harm to your equity when you start losing, you can also start with a smaller initial trade. Keep in mind that it takes longer to break even after losses than it does to lose the same amount.

Advanced Equity percent with stop loss

The idea behind this strategy is to restrict each transaction to a certain percentage of your overall account equity, which is often between 2 and 10%. This strategy is different from Fixed Ratio in that it protects your cumulative earnings while increasing your market exposure through the use of futures.

CHAPTER 3

Risks to watch out for in Forex Trading

When trading on the foreign exchange market, there are several dangers to take into consideration. With the appropriate risk management techniques, the majority of these dangers may be reduced.

The possibility of significant losses can be reduced with the use of sound risk management techniques. The following are some of the most typical trading hazards that you should be aware of:

Risk in Operations

This is a risk related to your trading platform's infrastructure and technology. This usually covers elements like the trading platform's dependence on external networks.

Liquidity Risk

This is a danger that might arise when a certain currency combination isn't available. This implies that there is a chance that at the moment of the deal, the currency's trade will be unavailable. With effective risk management, this risk may be reduced.

Danger of Lawsuit

This kind of risk entails breaking trade regulations within a nation. This may entail actions like passing legislation and regulations. It is your obligation as a forex trader to verify that your broker has a license so as to comply to national regulations. By dealing with an authorized broker who holds the necessary authorizations, this can be lessened.

Danger of the Market

The market's volatility is known as market risk. This involves issues like global relationships, financial issues, and instability in politics. Effective money management and risk management techniques help reduce market risks.

Country Risk

This is the danger that comes with dealing in a certain currency within a particular nation. This includes the danger of depending on a middleman in a nation dealing with political and economic unrest. Making sure you have a suitable broker in a nation you have investigated and determined to be politically and economically stable will help to lessen this.

Danger of Social Order

Social risk and the social problems that exist in a certain nation are related. This covers the possibility of societal instability as well as political, economic, and social problems. Selecting a broker from a nation whose reputation you can trust as well as its political and economic stability can help to reduce social risk.

Risk of interest rates

Forex prices may fluctuate significantly as they react to changes in the interest rate.

Danger of collapse

It is impossible to continue trading and produce the anticipated gains when trading cash is depleted.

What to do if you've lost a lot of money

Regardless of level of skill, many Forex traders frequently lose money. Common causes include inadequate money, aggressive trading, indecision, panic, absence of monitoring, and inadequate planning, in addition to inadequate risk management.

If you find yourself in such a circumstance, do the following actions:

- Remain composed and act with consideration to prevent more losses.
- Analyze your errors to learn from them to avoid repeated errors in future attempts.
- Recognize the harm, accept the loss, and create a trade plan.

- Give yourself time to heal gradually. Before going back to your regular trading, think about using demo accounts.

Never forget that Forex trading involves losses. Learn what you can from them to advance your career and sharpen your abilities.

CHAPTER 4

Essential Forex Trading Rule

Trade only funds you are ready to lose

Even though it should go without saying, the first rule of trading, whether it be Forex or anything else, is to never risk more money than you can afford to lose.

A lot of traders, particularly novices, disregard this guideline because they believe it "won't happen to them."

You wouldn't take all of your money to a casino to wager on black, isn't that true, if trading were same to gambling there? The same applies to trading: don't use the money you need to survive on unwarranted risks.

Why?

First, trading with money you don't have will put more strain and mental stress on you, which will make it harder for you to make decisions and raise the possibility that you won't make any profits at all.

Secondly, trading with money you don't have will make it more likely that you will make mistakes.

Because of the volatility of the foreign exchange markets, it is advisable to trade "conservative amounts" of your disposable income. Unfortunately, trading is not for you if you cannot afford to lose the money you are trading.

Always use stop-loss and limit orders

Orders are directives to your broker to initiate a transaction upon reaching a specific price threshold in the underlying market.

In order to exit a transaction if the market swings against you, stop-loss orders are put on open positions; this effectively "stops your loss."

You ought to place limit orders and stop losses on each transaction for the following three reasons:

• Protecting your downside is simple good sense.

• You have a more positive outlook and may step away from your trading screen with the knowledge that some protection is in place.

• You may use the method to compare the trade to your trading plan.

Consider your level of risk tolerance.

Knowing your level of risk tolerance is more than simply a way to reduce your worry about currency fluctuations or improve your quality of sleep at night. Knowing that you are in charge of the circumstance comes from the fact that you are exchanging the appropriate quantity of money in connection to your unique financial circumstances and your financial goals.

By trading within your risk tolerance, you may raise your chances of making money from the market.

Make sure that your risk to reward ratio is at least 1:2

Understanding the risk/reward ratio (RRR) and how to construct stop-loss and limit orders to safeguard your cash will undoubtedly increase your chances of long-term profitability.

The RRR calculates and evaluates the separation between your entry point and your take-profit and stop-loss orders.

Day traders and scalpers should strive for a minimum RRR of 1:2, while position and longer-term swing traders should aim for a broader minimum of 1:3.

Manage the risk associated with each trade

Additionally, you should set your trade risk at a cautious level and think about it as a proportion of your trading capital.

This is particularly crucial if you're new to trading and are likely to make more mistakes than an experienced trader.

A sensible beginning point would be to not risk more than 1% of your available money per trade. You should only risk a modest percentage of your trading capital per deal. Applying good RRR entails taking a 1% risk with a potential 3% return.

Maintain a constant level of risk

One of the easiest ways to blow up your account is for most novices to raise the size of their positions as soon as they start to make money. Maintain a constant level of risk.

It doesn't guarantee that your subsequent transaction will be lucrative just because you've made a few profitable ones.

Avoid being overconfident and less risk-averse since doing so will cause you to make rash decisions about your finances and risk management strategy.

You have to establish guidelines while creating your trading plan in order to determine the appropriate size for your positions. This is only the first step towards developing a profitable trading strategy; the next is to adhere to and execute your trading plan!

Recognize and manage leverage

Leveraged products include spread bets, CFDs, and spot forex, the three margin products we have covered so far in the course.

Thanks to margin trading, leverage allows you to trade with amounts greater than your original investment. Only a modest percentage of the whole amount of the position you wish to open as collateral will be required from you by your broker.

Using leverage can swiftly increase your earnings, but keep in mind that your losses will also be amplified in proportion.

For this reason, you should be aware of how margin trading and leverage operate, as well as how they affect your trading and overall success.

Forex traders are sometimes tempted to utilize high leverage in an attempt to generate significant profits, but if you are overleveraged, a small error or a sudden move in the market might result in a huge loss.

Consider currency correlation

It's critical to realize that currencies are tied to one another, or correlated, as they are valued in pairs.

By lowering total risks, understanding Forex correlations can help you better regulate the exposure of your Forex portfolio. A measure of how the price of one asset varies in relation to another is called correlation.

When two assets have a positive correlation, they tend to move in the same direction; conversely, when they have a negative correlation, they move in different ways.

You should keep the following in mind if you want to take advantage of foreign currency correlations:

- Do not open several trade that conflict with one another.

It's practically like having no trading position in your account if, for example, you go long on the EUR/USD and the USD/CHF. You may expect both currency pairs to grow in different directions.

Why?

Because the USD is utilized twice—once as the quote currency (EUR/USD) and once as the base currency (USD/CHF), the development of one exchange rate cancels out the other. Therefore, if the USD rises versus its main equivalents, the EUR/USD will rise and the USD/CHD would fall.

- Do not quote or open positions in the same base currency.

For example, you may anticipate positive correlation between the currency pairings GBP/USD, AUD/USD, and EUR/USD if you go long on them as they all have the same quotation currency, the USD.

It implies your portfolio will increase or decrease based on how strong or weak the USD is.

- Recognize the currencies of commodities

Because the nations they represent are mostly dependent on the export of these goods, commodity currencies are those that fluctuate in line with commodity prices.

The currencies of the companies that produce commodities will often increase in value if commodity prices rise, and vice versa.

CHAPTER 5

CONCLUSION

To be a good trader, you must first understand that forex traders are survivors first and lucrative second. Any trading method may turn a profit if you know how to manage your money and reduce risk.

In actuality, controlling your trading endeavors requires careful consideration of risk. Over time, you will not reap the full benefits of your method if you place too much risk on a single transaction. If you use all of the risk management techniques covered in earlier chapters, you should eventually see an increase in your success with forex trading.

Trading Forex pairs carries a high inherent risk. It varies according on a person's risk tolerance, but it can't be completely avoided. For this reason, managing Forex risk effectively through a plan and strategy is essential to limiting gains and losses.

Create a customized plan that is in line with your characteristics and goals. Remain calm, place stop losses, keep an eye on currency risk methodically, be realistic, and stick to a market-analysis-based Forex trading strategy.

When trading in the forex market, there is always a chance that you might lose money, no matter how hard you work at it. Recall that before you begin trading, you should have a set amount of money that you are willing to lose.

foreign exchange carries a wide range of dangers, all of which should be fully understood before investing. You'll be able to make a lot of money and stay safe using this. Always remember that prior knowledge is essential, particularly when attempting risk management.

But bear in mind that risk is always a component of trading foreign exchange, regardless of how much you study and prepare yourself. Nonetheless, risk can be minimized if you are aware of the dangers. Put another way, you can maximize your profits from trades and ensure that you are getting the highest return on your investment even if you end up losing money along the way.

GET INSTANT ACCESS TO THE FREE VIDEO COURSE BY FOLLOWING THE BELOW LINK

subscribepage.io/freeforexcourse

Click or copy and paste the above link on your browser for instant access to the bonus video.

www.ingramcontent.com/pod-product-compliance
Lightning Source LLC
Chambersburg PA
CBHW062250290526
45794CB00006B/2493